HATHA YOGA
FOR KIDS
by kids!

by the Children of Yogaville

Other Books from Integral Yoga Publications

Books by Sri Swami Satchidananda

Beyond Words
The Golden Present (Daily Readings)
Guru and Disciple
The Healthy Vegetarian
Integral Yoga Hatha

Kailash Journal
The Living Gita
Satchidananda Sutras
To Know Your Self
The Yoga Sutras of Patanjali

Books about Swami Satchidananda

Boundless Giving: The Life and Service of Sri Swami Satchidananda
Sri Swami Satchidananda: Apostle of Peace
Sri Swami Satchidananda: Portrait of a Modern Sage
The Master's Touch

Other Books for Children

Imagine That–A Child's Guide to Yoga
Meditating with Children
Meditation for Children
Sparkling Together
Enlightening Tales

Other Books

Bound to Be Free
Dictionary of Sanskrit Names
Everybody's Vegan Cookbook
Inside the Yoga Sutras
LOTUS Prayer Book

Library of Congress Cataloging-in-Publication Data:

Hatha Yoga for Kids, by Kids!/by the Children of Yogaville.
p.cm.
Summary: Instructional photographs and simple text written by children introduce the basic, optional, and meditative poses of Hatha Yoga.
ISBN 978-0-932040-36-7
1. Yoga, Hatha Yoga for Children—Juvenile literature. 2. Children's writings. (1.Yoga.
2. Children's writings.) 1.Title.
RA781.7.C475 1990
613.7'046'083—dc2O

90-46679
CIP
AC

Second Printing 2000   third printing 2013

Integral Yoga® Publications
Satchidananda Ashram-Yogaville, Inc, Buckingham, Virginia 23921

www.yogaville.org

Printed in the United States of America.
Design and layout: Prema Joseffe Conan
Photography: Ganesh MacIsaac, Rhagavan Rood, Swami Sharadananda Ma, Swami Tyagananda

DEDICATION

To Sri Gurudev, Swami Satchidanandaji Maharaj,
who has brought to light the ancient teachings
of the Science of Yoga and
made it available to children of all ages.

TABLE OF CONTENTS

INTRODUCTION: TO PARENTS

Health, not disease, is our birthright. Strength, not weakness, is our heritage. Courage, but not fear. Peace, but not restlessness. Knowledge, but not ignorance. Bliss, but not sorrow.

Certainly we all want our children to realize and appreciate their heritage and birthright. Children come into this world very pure, and it is up to the adults to help them stay bright, strong, and healthy.

There is no better health tonic than Yoga asanas. The asanas are effective in the prevention of disease and in aiding the cure of existing disease as well. From prince to peasant, child to grandparent, ailing to robust, all can practice these Yoga poses with maximum advantage.

Remember, the best way to learn is by example. So set a good example for your children. If they see you doing something, they will want to imitate it. If they watch you doing Yoga asanas, they will want to join in. Likewise, if they see you smoking a cigarette, they will want to try that too. No matter how you advise them, if you yourself have unhealthy habits, the children will follow.

And, of course, it's very important not to force the children to practice Yoga. You know how *you* rebelled if your parents tried to force a practice or religion or a certain way on you.

Simply talk with your child about the benefits, let him or her see you doing it regularly, and make it fun.

These young angels who put together this book have found it to be fun, and they can beautifully show that to other children.

To the children of all ages, I wish you enjoyment and success in your practice of Yoga. May you attain your birthright, your Divine Heritage, to shine as fully developed Yogis—radiating joy, peace, and knowledge everywhere.

OM Shanthi Shanthi Shanthi

Sri Swami Satchidananda

INTRODUCTION: TO CHILDREN

My beloved children, you all know that everyone wants to be happy and strong. And in order to really have success and fun in this world, you need to be healthy. The Yoga practices in this book will help you to *be* that way and to *stay* that way.

The children who worked on this book have all done these practices for years. They have told me how much they enjoy Yoga and that it helps them to feel healthy and good about themselves.

Yoga is good for everyone, so practice well. Then you can say to your parents and your friends, "Come on. Try this with me!" But don't try to force your friends to do it. Let them see how much fun *you* have, and they themselves will want to do it too.

May these great Yoga practices help you to enjoy wonderful health and happiness and to shine as beautiful beacons of light in the world.

OM Shanthi Shanthi Shanthi. OM Peace Peace Peace.

Sri Swami Satchidananda

THE GOAL OF INTEGRAL YOGA

The Goal of Integral Yoga and the birthright of every individual is to realize the spiritual unity behind all the diversities of the entire creation and to live harmoniously as members of one universal family. This goal is achieved by maintaining our mutual condition of a body of optimum health and strength; senses under total control; a mind well-disciplined, clear, and calm; an intellect as sharp as a razor; a will as strong and pliable as steel; a heart full of unconditional love and compassion; an ego as pure as crystal; and a life filled with Supreme Peace and Joy.

Sri Swami Satchidananda

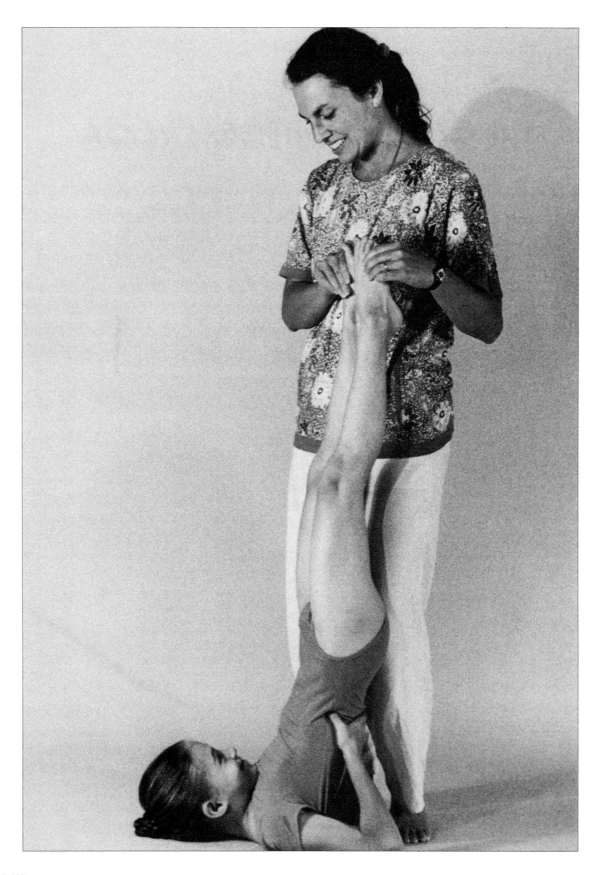

XII

NOTES TO PARENTS

In guiding children to do the Hatha Yoga poses, gentleness and care are very important. Children's bodies are still growing; not all the parts are fully developed, and extra precautions are needed so that no strain occurs. If they are unsteady in a pose, it's best for them to come out, rest, and go on to another pose. If an asana cannot be held as long as is normally done, they can repeat it several times until they hold it for the suggested time. If you observe how your children do in the poses and make any necessary adaptations, you should be able to develop a very beneficial and enjoyable routine. By inspiring and guiding your young ones to do these practices, you will be giving them a very great gift — a strong foundation for their future health and happiness.

Age: The children in this book are from five to twelve years old. The basic class given here is mainly for children of these ages. After twelve years usually a child can begin the adult beginners class (see *Integral Yoga Hatha*).

Children under five can easily try many of these poses, but don't expect them to hold the poses or to maintain the exact form. They will have fun imitating their older brothers and sisters.

Beginners: Beginners should not be in a hurry to do the pose in its perfect position. It is very important that each child practice to his own capacity and not strain in any pose. These poses are not for competition.

Time: It is important to wait at least two hours after eating before beginning Hatha Yoga practice.

Parents may find deep relaxation at bedtime is very helpful for children who have trouble falling asleep.

Diet: Although there are no "musts" about diet, you will see maximum benefit for your child if you feed him/her a pure and plain, vegetarian diet avoiding meat, fish, and eggs. Also it would be of great benefit to reduce sugar and "junk food" in the children's diet.

Please wait about a half hour after practicing before eating a light snack and one hour for a full meal.

Games and Physical Exercises: It is advisable not to mix vigorous games and exercises with Hatha Yoga practices. It is best to have the more vigorous activity first. After a sufficient rest, begin the Yoga practices.

Inspiration: The best way to motivate your children in Yoga practice is to be an example yourself. It is our intention that any child who looks at the photos in this book will see that the kids are having fun as well as accomplishing some difficult poses. We hope that just looking at the book will make other children want to try the poses. But for a regular practice you will need to set aside a certain quiet time to guide your child through the practices. Never force them, but use loving guidance, supported by your good example.

May All Be Filled With Peace and Joy, Love and Light.

All instructions and comments on the poses are written by the children in this book.

Section I

SOORYA NAMASKAR
SALUTATION TO THE SUN.

SOORYA NAMASKAR - SALUTATION TO THE SUN.

Salutation to the Sun is a series of twelve poses done as one continuous movement. You can do it slowly, stretching well in each position and breathing deeply. This helps to calm the mind. You can also do it very fast like a drill. This wakes you up!

We always do three to four rounds before beginning the Hatha Yoga poses.

Benefits:

Salutation to the Sun stretches the entire body and gets you ready for the other poses.

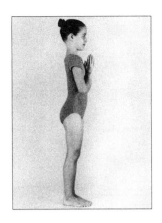  

POSITION 1

Please stand up straight with your feet together and your palms together at your chest. Look straight ahead of you.

POSITION 2

Lock your thumbs together. Stretch your arms straight up above your head so that your arms are in line with your head next to your ears. Stretch toward the ceiling.

POSITION 3

Please stretch forward toward your feet, and try to touch your toes. Bring your forehead toward your knees. Keep your knees straight.

POSITION 4

Please put your hands flat on the floor next to your feet. Bend your legs if you need to. Stretch your left leg back, and bring your left knee to the floor. Keep your right foot flat on the floor between your hands, and look up toward the ceiling.

POSITION 5

Please bring your right leg back next to the left leg. Raise your bottom up in the air. The only part of your body that is touching the floor should be your feet and palms. Look toward the feet. Stretch your heels down toward the floor. Your body will make a triangle shape.

POSITION 6

Bring your knees, chest, and chin to the floor. Leave your bottom raised up a little. Have your palms flat on the floor under your shoulders. Be sure to have your feet together.

SOORYA NAMASKAR - SALUTATION TO THE SUN _____ 9

POSITION 7

Lower your bottom, and raise your head and chest slowly off the floor. Keep your stomach on the floor. Don't use your hands to push your back up. Keep your feet together.

POSITION 8

Now raise your bottom in the air with your arms and legs straight. Your palms and soles of your feet should be the only part of your body touching the floor. Look back toward the knees. This is the triangle position again.

POSITION 9

Now bring your left leg forward between the palms. Have your right knee on the floor. Look up toward the ceiling.

POSITION 10

Bring your right foot forward next to your left foot. Straighten your legs. Try to touch your toes. Drop your head down, and let your arms hang down.

SOORYA NAMASKAR - SALUTATION TO THE SUN _____ 13

POSITION 11

Now lock your thumbs together. Stretch up toward the ceiling with your arms along side the head. Look straight ahead of you.

POSITION 12

Now have your palms together at your chest. Relax. Do three to four rounds of all 12 positions, then lie on your back, and relax.

Section II

BASIC HATHA YOGA POSES

BASIC HATHA YOGA POSES

These nine poses along with deep relaxation are the basic Hatha Yoga Poses, or Cultural Poses. Just doing these few poses daily can keep you in good health. They should be done in the order given. You can add any optional poses you want before Yoga Mudra and deep relaxation.

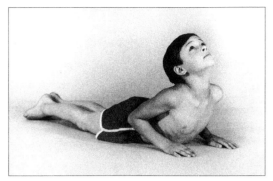

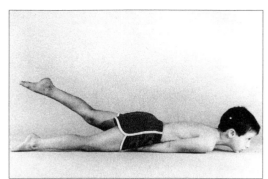

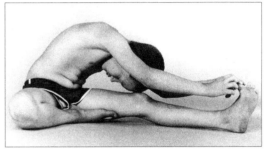

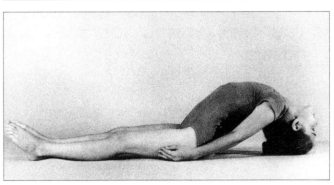

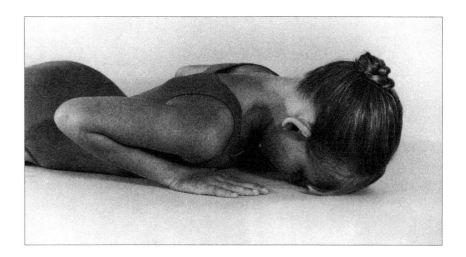

BHUJANGASANA - COBRA POSE

First, you lie on your stomach. Then you put your feet together. Place your forehead on the floor, and put the palms of your hands on the floor underneath your shoulders. Very, very slowly raise your head and chest up as far as you can go without putting weight on your hands and without lifting your belly button off the floor. You should be looking up toward the ceiling. Stay in that position as long as you can without straining. Before you start to strain, slowly lower your chest and your head. First, bring your chest to the floor. Then bring your forehead to the floor. Put your arms down at your sides. Spread your feet about a foot apart, and relax.

Benefits:

Cobra Pose stretches your upper spine and back in a way that they usually don't get stretched. It also makes the spine strong.

BHUJANGASANA - COBRA POSE _____ **21**

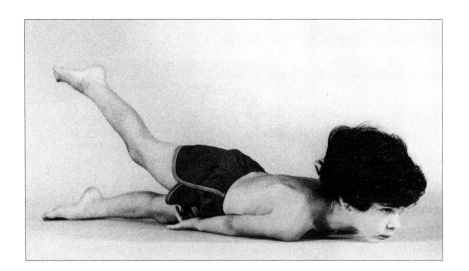

ARDDHA SALABASANA - HALF-LOCUST POSE

First, lie on your stomach. Then put your feet together and your chin on the floor in front of you. Then put your arms under your stomach with your palms up. Don't cross or bend your arms. After that, very slowly raise your right leg a foot or two above the floor. Don't bend your knee. Stay in that position for as long as you can without straining. Before you start to strain, lower your right leg, and relax it. Then raise your left leg, and hold it for as long as you held up the right leg. Then repeat, doing each leg again. After that, take your arms out from underneath your stomach. Turn your palms up. Then spread your feet about a foot apart. Turn your head to the side, and relax.

Benefits:

This pose stretches your lower back and makes it strong.

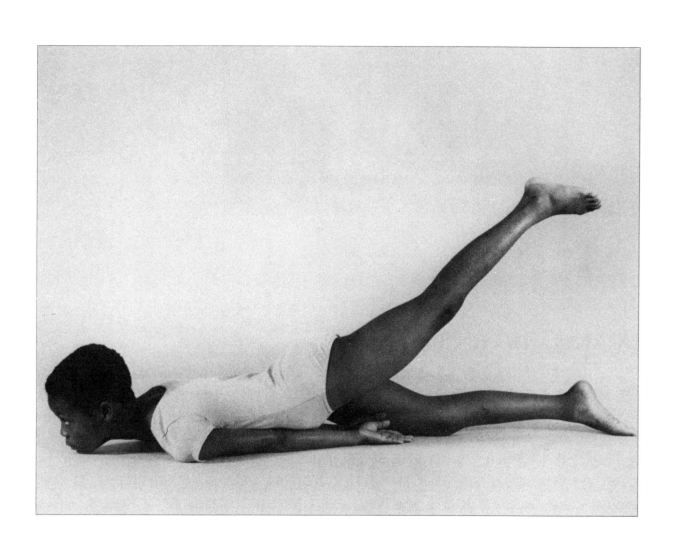

ARDDHA SALABASANA - HALF-LOCUST POSE _____ **23**

SALABASANA - LOCUST POSE

Lie on your stomach. Put your feet together and your chin on the floor in front of you. Then put your arms under your stomach with your palms up. Don't cross or bend your arms. Raise both legs about a foot off the floor with knees straight, and hold this position for as long as you can without straining. Before you start straining, slowly lower your legs to the floor. You can repeat this 2 to 3 times. After that spread your legs about a foot apart, take your arms out from under you, and turn your head to the side. Then relax.

Benefits:

The Locust Pose helps your lower back and pelvis.

SALABASANA - LOCUST POSE

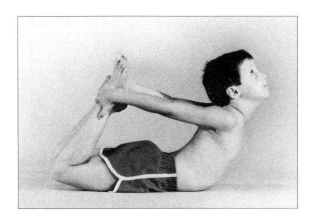

DHANURASANA - BOW POSE

Please lie flat on your stomach with your feet together. Have your forehead on the floor. Bend your legs, and hold on to your ankles with your hands. Keep your arms straight. Try to keep your legs and feet together. Now slowly raise both halves of the body, leaving only your stomach on the floor if possible. Keep your head back. Look up and back. Try to stay in the pose for 10 seconds. If you can't and the pose strains your body, come down sooner. When coming out of the pose, slowly let your body come down to the floor. Your body should be totally relaxed. Slowly turn your head to the side. Let your arms come down to your sides, palms up. Now let your legs come flat down to the floor. You can now move your feet apart, about a foot. Relax.

Benefits:

This pose benefits your whole body, especially your entire spine and abdomen.

DHANURASANA - BOW POSE _____ 27

JANUSIRSHASANA - HEAD-TO-KNEE POSE

Lie on your back with your arms by your sides with your palms up and your feet spread about a foot apart. Then put your feet together, and raise your arms above your head. Then lock your thumbs together, and slowly sit up. Next keep your right leg straight, and bend the left leg so that the bottom of the left foot is touching the right thigh. Then slowly bend forward over your right leg, and try to bring your forehead to your knee without bending your knee. If you can't reach the knee, then just bend forward as much as possible. Do not strain. Hold on to your leg or foot with both hands. Before you start to strain, slowly raise up, and stretch the back up. Then do the left leg in the same way. After that, raise your arms and back so that you're sitting straight up with your arms straight above your head with your fingertips pointing to the ceiling. Have both legs straight out in front of you. Then lower your back and arms to the floor. Put your arms to your sides, and spread your feet about a foot apart. Then relax.

Benefits:

This pose stretches the lower back and the back of the legs. It also squeezes the abdomen.

JANUSIRSHASANA - HEAD-TO-KNEE POSE _____ 29

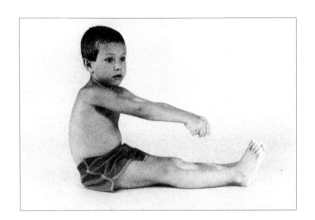 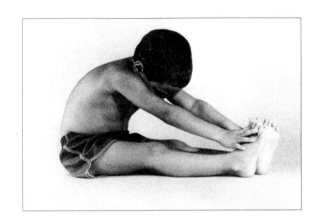

PASCHIMOTHANASANA - FORWARD-BENDING POSE

Please lie flat on your back with your feet together. Keep your head and legs straight. Now stretch your arms over your head, keeping them straight. Lock your thumbs together. Now slowly sit up. Your arms should be straight up. Feel like you're reaching toward the ceiling. Now stretch forward. Try to touch your feet with your hands. If you can't, that's fine. Just come down as far as you can, and hold on to your legs with your hands. Let your head drop forward, and relax in the pose. Try to stay in the pose for 20 seconds. If you can't stay that long, come up sooner. When coming out of this pose, slowly sit up, and roll your back down to the floor. Put your arms to your sides. Spread your feet apart about a foot. Relax.

Benefits:

This pose benefits your back, the back of your legs, and the stomach area.

PASCHIMOTHANASANA - FORWARD-BENDING POSE _____ *31*

HALASANA - PLOW POSE

Please lie flat on your back. Have your feet together and your arms along side your body with your palms down. Move your hair to the side so that it's not behind your neck (if you have long hair). Keep your head straight. Now slowly raise your legs up straight in the air so that the soles of your feet are toward the ceiling. Keeping your legs together, bring your legs all the way over your head - until the feet touch the floor. (If your feet do not come to the floor, just go straight up into shoulder stand.) Don't bend your knees. Curl your toes under. Be sure you're not straining. Stay in the pose as long as it's comfortable. Slowly let your legs come down to the floor. Be sure not to bend your knees while coming down to the floor. Now just relax in corpse pose (Savasana).

Benefits:

This pose benefits your spine and back muscles. It keeps the spine flexible.

HALASANA - PLOW POSE _____ 33

SARVANGASANA - ALL MEMBERS POSE, SHOULDER STAND

Lie flat on your back with your feet together and your arms touching your sides. Put your palms facing down. Next, raise your legs together so that they come over your head and your bottom comes up off the floor. Don't strain and don't bend your knees. When your legs are over your head, bend your elbows so that your hands are supporting your back. Then raise your legs so that the bottoms of your feet face the ceiling. Your legs and back should be in a straight line, and your chin should be touching your upper chest. Stay in this position for as long as possible without straining. Before you start to strain, slowly lower your legs over your head, and bring your arms down so that they are flat on the floor. Bring your legs slowly down until your bottom is on the floor and your legs are straight up. Slowly lower your legs down with the knees straight. Spread your legs about a foot apart, and bring your arms about four inches away from your sides. Then relax.

Danger!:

Do not turn your head and look around in Shoulder Stand. You might hurt your neck badly.

Benefits:

This pose helps every part of your body. That's why it is called the All Members Pose.

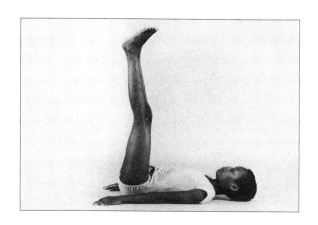

SARVANGASANA - ALL MEMBERS POSE
SHOULDER STAND _____ **35**

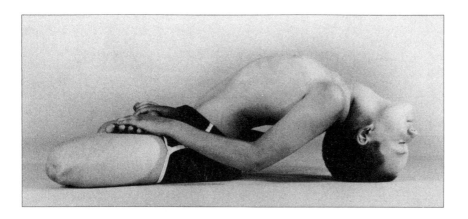

MATSYASANA - FISH POSE

Please lie flat on your back with your feet together. Have your palms pressing against the sides of your thighs. Sit half-way up, leaning on your elbows so that you can see your feet. Keep your legs straight. Arch your back, and put the crown of your head on the floor. Smile slightly keeping your mouth closed. Close your eyes. Your upper back should come off the floor, and your seat should stay on the floor. Have some nice, slow, deep breathing. Stay in this pose as long as you can without straining any part of your body. When coming up out of this pose, slowly lift your head first. Use your elbows to help lift your head off the floor. Now lower your back and head down to the floor. Keep your head centered on the floor. Let your arms come down to your sides. Spread your feet apart about a foot. Relax.

Note:

Always do this pose after shoulder stand. It stretches the neck in the opposite direction.

Benefits:

It stretches the neck muscles and opens your lungs fully.

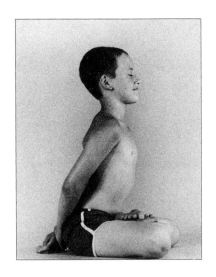 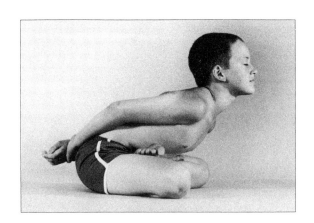

YOGA MUDRA - YOGIC SEAL

First, sit in a comfortable, cross-legged position with your back straight. Slowly bring your arms behind your back, and hold onto your right wrist with your left hand. Breathe in. Then slowly breathe out. While you are breathing out, slowly bend forward as far as you can without straining. Do not raise your seat off the floor. When you are as far down as you can go, drop your head. Bring the forehead to the floor, or if it's comfortable, bring the chin to the floor. Stay in that position for ten seconds or more. To come out of this pose, stretch your chin forward, and breathe in deeply. When you breathe in, slowly come up and sit up straight. Then slowly bring your hands to your lap, and sit like that with your eyes closed, being perfectly still for ten seconds, feeling the peaceful vibrations.

Benefits:

This pose should always be done last because it seals in all the energy you get from doing Hatha Yoga, and it also helps your abdominal muscles.

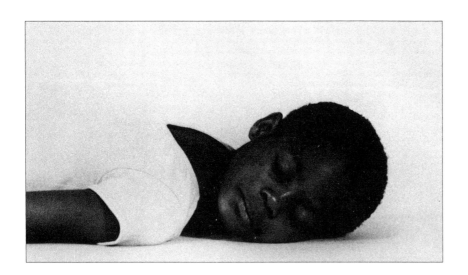

SAVASANA - CORPSE POSE - to be done after each pose

The Corpse Pose is a relaxing pose. Please lie flat on your back with your feet about a foot apart. Have your head centered with your arms away from the body and your palms facing up. Close your eyes, and relax. Try to slow your breathing.

Benefits

This pose benefits your whole body and calms your mind.

Relaxation on the Abdomen

Lie on your stomach with your cheek turned to the side. Have your feet apart about one foot and your arms at the sides with your palms up. Have your eyes closed. This is good to do after each backward bending pose.

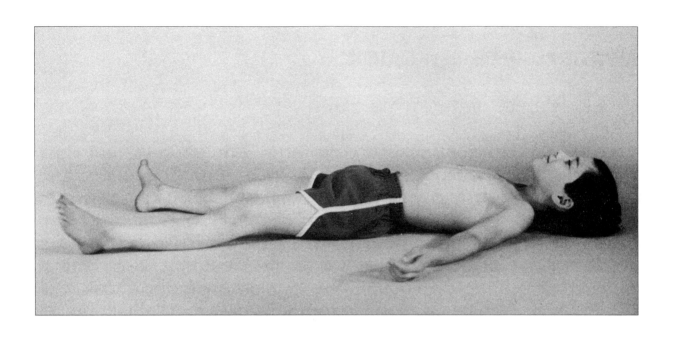

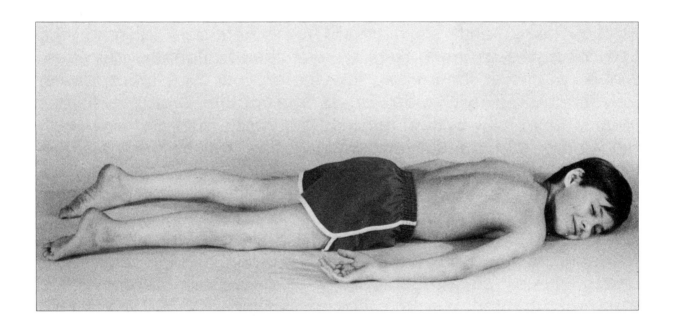

SAVASANA - DEEP RELAXATION

This is done at the end of all the poses.

Please lie flat on your back in corpse pose. First, tense up your right leg, lift it up off the floor a few inches, squeeze for 5 seconds, and drop it. Roll your leg from side to side, and forget it. Do the same with your left leg. Tense up your bottom for 7 seconds while holding your breath. Relax, and forget about it. Take a big breath in, and fill your stomach with air. Puff it up like a balloon for 5 seconds. Relax, letting all the air burst out of your mouth. Take in a deep breath, and fill your chest with air. Stay like that for 7 seconds. Relax again, letting the air out of the mouth. Tense up your right arm, squeeze your right hand into a fist, raise it off the floor, and hold for 5 seconds. Drop it, and relax. Do the same with the left arm. Lift your shoulders up toward your ears and chin, tense, and hold for 5 seconds. Let them drop to the floor. Relax. Gently roll your head from side to side. Squeeze your face all up like a prune. Suck in your cheeks. Tighten your eyes. Wrinkle your nose. Then relax. Now stretch your face the opposite way. Open your eyes wide. Open your mouth. Stretch out your tongue. Relax. Now without moving your body, mentally relax each part starting from the toes and going up the body to the top of the head. Just forget about the body now. Watch your breath, and see how it is slowing down. Now watch your thoughts. Just let your thoughts slowly fade away. Relax. Keep in this state of deep relaxation for 5 to 10 minutes. Then take in a slow deep breath, and you will begin to feel a tingling sensation moving through your body, waking you up. You can gently begin to stretch out. You can slowly sit up in a comfortable cross-legged position. You will feel totally relaxed and refreshed.

Benefits:

Totally relaxes and refreshes the body and mind.

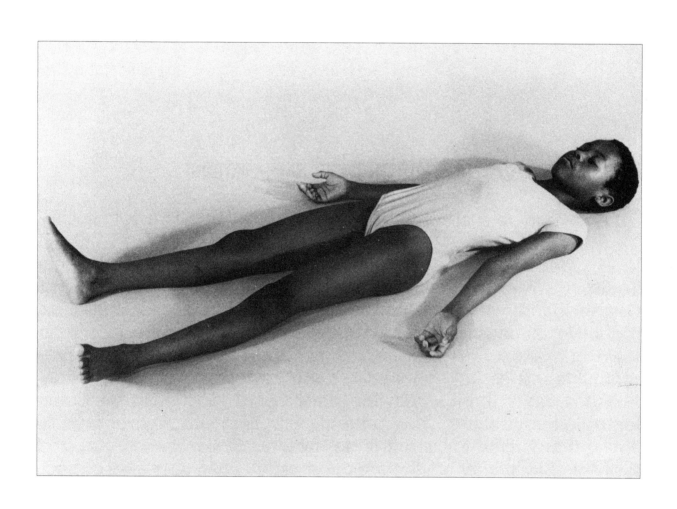

SEEGRA SAVASANA - QUICK DEEP RELAXATION

(This pose can be done instead of deep relaxation if time is limited.)

Lie on your back in Savasana (Corpse Pose). Then take a deep breath in. While you hold your breath, tense your entire body and raise up so that you are balancing on your buttocks. Stay like this for about five seconds, and really squeeze everything tightly. Then drop down and relax. Roll your legs, arms, and head from side to side about three times. Relax the entire body, and do not move. Mentally relax the body. Then watch the breath and mind as in the Deep Relaxation instructions. Stay perfectly still, and watch your breath. Stay in this position for about three minutes. Slowly stretch out, and slowly sit up with your back perfectly straight. Keep your eyes closed, and chant the word OM three times. After you do Seegra Savasana, (Quick Deep Relaxation) you should feel totally refreshed.

Benefits:

This pose totally relaxes and refreshes your entire body. It should be done after finishing all your asanas.

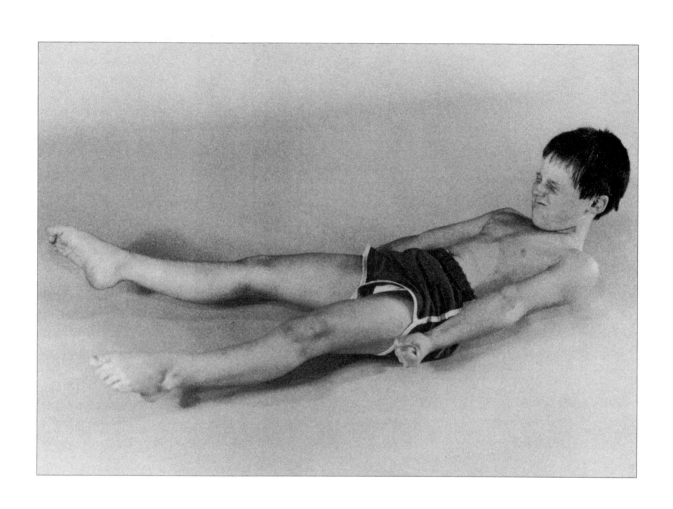

Section III

OPTIONAL POSES

OPTIONAL POSES

This section shows some more difficult poses. It is for those who have more time to practice and like greater variety. They should be done before Yoga Mudra and Deep Relaxation.

These poses do not have to be done in any certain order, so they are listed alphabetically.

We have not listed particular benefits because by doing them you will find the benefit yourself.

Have fun, and please don't strain.

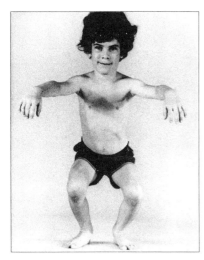  

BADDHA PADMASANA - BOUND LOTUS POSE

First, sit in Lotus Pose (see Meditative Poses—Section IV). Wrap your right arm around your back, and hold onto the big toe of your right foot. Wrap your left arm around your back on top of the right arm, and hold onto your big toe of your left foot. Then sit up very straight.

When you are beginning this pose, you can try doing one side at a time, alternating sides.

"This pose is hard, but it really made me feel great when I finally did it!"

BADDHA YOGA MUDRA - BOUND YOGA MUDRA

Sit in Bound Lotus Pose. Now close your eyes. Slowly bend forward, and touch the floor with your forehead or your chin. Stay in this pose as long as comfortable. Then slowly come up, and sit up straight.

"This pose makes me feel good. It was hard for me at first, but I watched my friends and tried it. I practiced and got it."

BADDHA PADMASANA - BOUND LOTUS POSE _____ 51

BADRASANA - GENTLE POSE

First, sit with your back straight. Then put the bottoms of your feet together on the floor in front of you. Next, lock your fingers together, and place them around your toes. Then slide your feet in as close to your seat as possible without straining. Then push your knees down without using your hands or arms. Be careful not to push your knees down too far because you could really hurt your legs. Stay in this position for as long as it is comfortable. When you start getting uncomfortable, you should shake out your legs.

"I like Gentle Pose because it stretches my legs, and it is fun. It helps you to do a better Lotus Pose."

BADRASANA - GENTLE POSE _____
53

CHAKRASANA - WHEEL POSE

Please lie flat on your back. Have your head centered. Have your feet about a foot apart. Now bend both your legs so that your knees are facing toward the ceiling. Have the soles of your feet flat on the floor. Your feet should be about a foot away from your bottom. Now bend your arms, and have your palms flat and straight next to your ears. Raise your body off the floor, arching your back. Your whole body should be off the floor except your palms and soles. This is one of the poses that you have to balance in. Stay in this pose as long as you can without straining any part of your body. If you can, straighten your arms. Try to stay in this pose for 20 seconds. If it strains your body to stay in this long, come down sooner. If you are comfortable, you can try to walk your hands and feet closer together until they meet. Now come down out of this pose–very slowly. You can now lie flat on your back and relax.

"This pose is a lot of fun and really makes you feel strong."

CHAKRASANA - WHEEL POSE _____ *55*

DURVASASANA - DURVASA'S POSE

Please sit on the floor with your legs straight out in front of you. Then take your right leg, and lift it up over your head, resting it on the back of your neck. Then put your palms down on the floor next to you, and rise up. Stand up on your left leg, bend the knee, and balance. Bring your palms together at your chest. Stay in this pose as long as you are comfortable. Then bring your palms down and your right leg back to the floor. Do the same pose with your left leg raised up.

"I like to do Durvasa's Pose because it is hard to do, and it looks so great."

EKA PADA TRIKONASANA - SINGLE-LEG TRIANGLE POSE

Sit with legs out straight. Hold onto your right foot, and raise it over your head. Stretch your left leg to the right side, and keep your palms flat on the floor on the sides of the body. Press on the palms, and lift up the left foot and body. Press the left toes into the floor, and put your right hand on the left knee.

DURVASASANA - DURVASA'S POSE

EKA PADA TRIKONASANA - SINGLE-LEG TRIANGLE POSE _____ 57

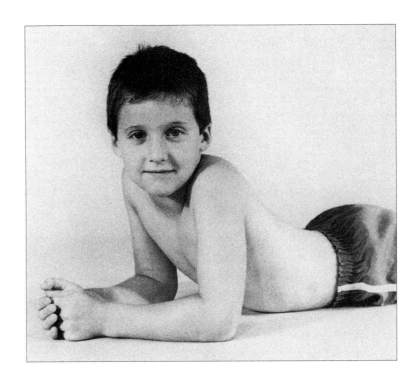

EKAPADHASIRSHASANA - LEG-TO-HEAD POSE

Please sit on the floor with your legs straight out in front of you. Then take your right leg, and lift it up over your head, resting it on the back of your neck. Bring your palms together at your chest. Stay in this pose as long as you can. Then bring your palms down and your right leg back to the floor. Do the same with your left leg.

"I like the Leg-to-Head Pose because it is so relaxing."

EKAPADHASIRSHASANA - LEG-TO-HEAD POSE _____ 59

GARUDASANA - EAGLE POSE

Please stand straight up with your feet together. Have your head centered. Concentrate on one point in front of you. Now lift up your right leg, and wrap it around your left leg so that it bends your left knee. You will be standing only on your left leg and foot. Wrap both arms around each other so that your palms come together at your left cheek. Try to stay in this pose for 30 seconds. If you can't, come down sooner. Stay up longer if you can. Now come out of this pose. Do this same pose with the left leg, having the arms and the palms together at your right cheek. You're pretty much reversing sides. Now come out of this pose, and relax.

Balancing Poses really take a lot of concentration. It helps to stare at one point in front of you.

GARUDASANA - EAGLE POSE _____ 61

GOMUKHASANA - COW-FACE POSE

Please get into the Heroic Pose (see the Meditative Poses, Section IV.) First, put your right arm behind your back so that it goes over the shoulder. Then with your left arm reach behind underneath your shoulder, and clasp your hands together behind your back. Keep your head up straight. Your whole body should be in a straight line from your knees up. Stay in this pose however long it feels comfortable. Now reverse sides having the left arm up and over the shoulder and the right arm under. Relax on your knees when you're finished.

If your hands don't reach, you can hold onto a cloth with both hands.

GOMUKHASANA - COW-FACE POSE _____ 63

KAKASANA - CROW POSE

Squat down on your toes. Put your palms flat on the floor in front of you about a foot away from your knees. Bend your elbows slightly. Now raise your knees so that they are resting on your elbows. Gently lean forward until your toes rise off the floor and you are balancing on your hands. Keep your head centered and facing forward. Be careful not to fall on your nose. Try to stay in this pose for 20 seconds or less. If you get really good at this pose, you can stay in it for a longer period. Now slowly come down out of this pose. Relax.

"This pose is a lot of fun and makes your arms very strong."

KAKASANA - CROW POSE _____ 65

KUKKUTASANA - COCK POSE

Please sit in the full lotus pose (see Meditation Poses, Section IV). Put your hands and wrists through the opening between your calves and thighs. Put your hands flat on the floor. Lift your body off the floor. All of your weight should be supported by your hands, wrists, and arm muscles. Look straight ahead of you with your head straight. Stay in this pose as long as you can without straining any part of your body. Now slowly let your body come down to the floor. Put your hands on your lap. Relax.

NATARAJASANA - KING DANCER POSE

Please stand up straight with your arms to your sides. Look straight ahead, and concentrate on one thing in front of you. This will help you to balance. Have your head centered. Put your weight on your left foot. Now bend your right knee. Hold onto your right ankle with your right hand. Keep your arms straight. Now lift your left arm up straight and balance in this pose. When you have mastered this position, you can try to bend forward so that your arm is straight out in front of you and your leg and back are arched. Stay in this pose as long as you can without straining any part of your body. Now come down slowly out of this pose. Let your leg come down to the floor. Let your arms drop down to your sides. Relax. Now do the same pose, standing on your right leg and raising the right arm.

NATARAJASANA - KING DANCER POSE _____ 69

POORNA NAUASANA - BACKWARD BOAT POSE

Please lie flat on your stomach with your feet together. Have your forehead on the floor. Stretch your arms straight in front of you. Lock your thumbs together, and keep your arms fairly close to your ears, head between your arms. Look straight ahead of you. Now slowly raise both halves of the body off the floor. You should be balancing on your abdomen. Your body will form a curve. Stay in the pose as long as you can without straining any part of your body. Now slowly come down out of this pose. Relax.

It takes a lot of strength to really curve, so be careful.

POORNA NAUASANA - BACKWARD BOAT POSE _____ *71*

SANKATASANA - CHAIR POSE

Stand with your feet about one foot apart. Put your arms out in front of you with the hands hanging loose. Bend your knees, and lower down. Imagine you are sitting on an invisible chair. Just sit down in mid-air, and hold it as long as you can.

You will really feel the muscles in your upper legs. This is good for bicycling.

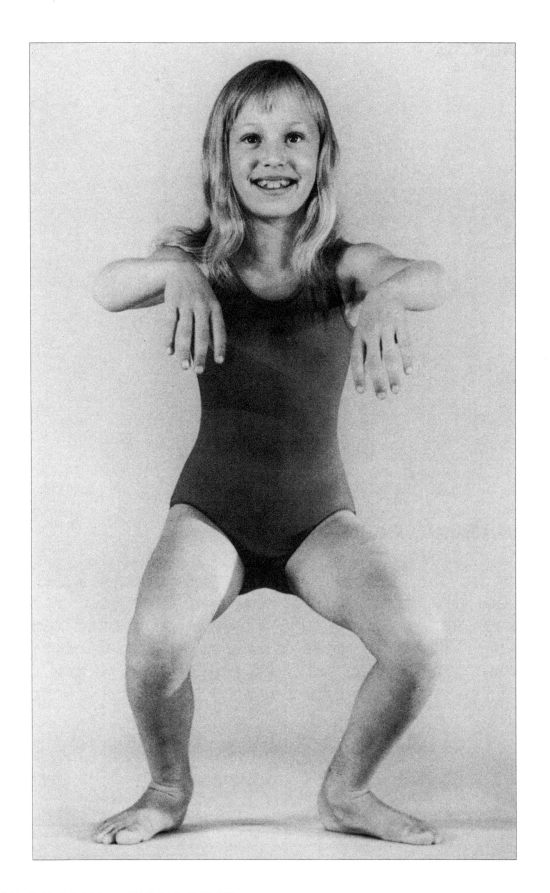

SANKATASANA - CHAIR POSE _____ 73

SASANGASANA - RABBIT POSE

Please sit on your knees with your toes curled under. Stand up on your knees. Keep concentrated. Now hold on to your ankles with your hands. Arch your back, and drop your head back. Keep your arms straight. Stay in this pose as long as you can without getting dizzy. When you come up out of this pose, very slowly raise up one arm at a time so you won't fall forward. You can now sit flat on your knees.

SASANGASANA - RABBIT POSE _____ *75*

SETHU BANDHA SARVANGASANA - BRIDGE SHOULDER STAND

Lie on your back. Now come up into shoulder stand (Sarvangasana). Hold your back with your hands. Bend the knees. (You can do one at a time or both together.) Bring the feet to the floor. Have the feet flat on the floor about one foot apart.

If you can, try raising the legs back into shoulder stand, and then come down.

SETHU BANDHA SARVANGASANA - BRIDGE SHOULDER STAND _ 77

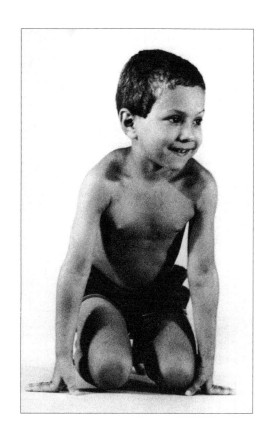

SIMHASANA - LION POSE

First, sit in Pelvic Pose (see Meditative Poses, Section IV) with your hands relaxed on your knees. Then all at once, let out all your breath, suck in your stomach, spread your fingers as wide apart as you can, straighten your arms, look up cross-eyed, touch your chin with the tip of your tongue, and roar! Stay in this position for ten to fifteen seconds. Then sit back, and relax in Pelvic Pose.

"I like this pose because it relaxes and refreshes me."

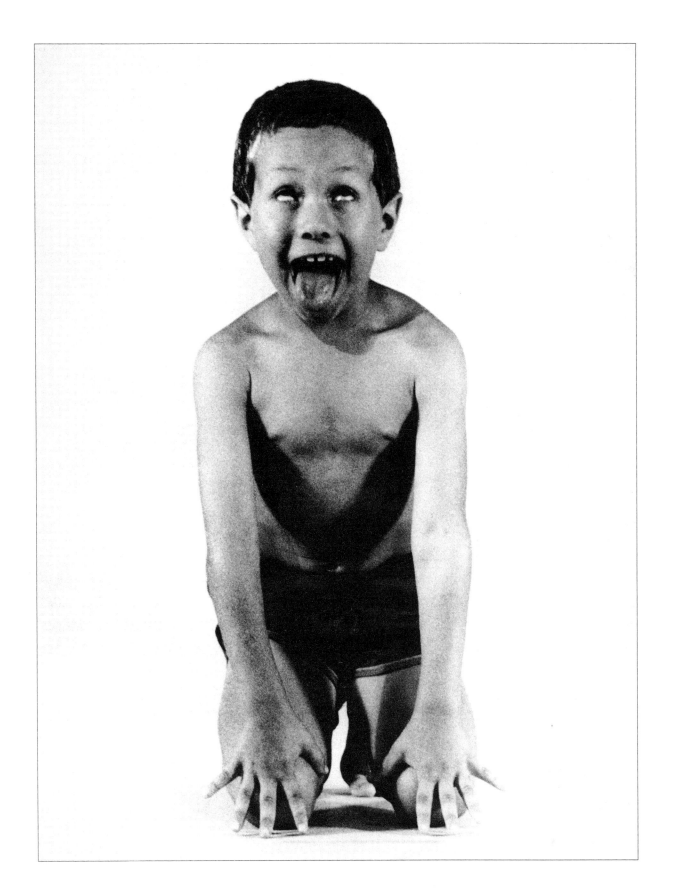

SIMHASANA - LION POSE _____ *79*

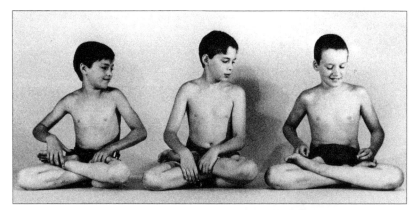

UTTHITHA PADMASANA - LIFTED LOTUS POSE

First, sit in the Lotus Pose (see Meditative Poses, Section IV). Then put your palms flat on the floor beside your outer thighs. Now push down with your hands. Slowly lift yourself off the floor with your hands. Hold this pose for as long as it is comfortable. Then slowly come back to the floor, and relax.

"What I like about this pose is that it's the easiest pose that strengthens your arms."

UTTHITHA PADMASANA - LIFTED LOTUS POSE _____ *81*

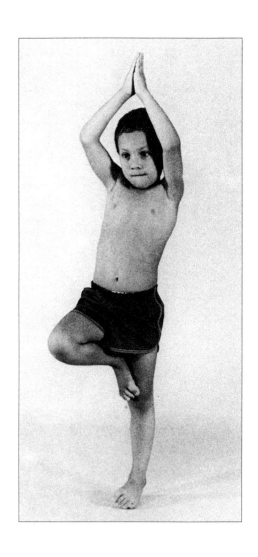

VRIKSHASANA - TREE POSE

Stand up on your right foot. Bring your left foot up so that the ankle is on top of your right thigh, or put the sole of the left foot on the inside of the right thigh. Put the palms together in front of the chest. Balance well. Slowly raise your hands above your head (your palms should still be together). Spread your arms out like the branches of a tree. Have your elbows straight. Come out of the pose slowly, and repeat using the left leg.

"I like Tree Pose because it helps me balance."

VRIKSHASANA - TREE POSE _____ **83**

YOGA NIDRASANA - YOGIC SLEEP POSE

Please lie flat on your back. Bring both of your legs up behind your head. Cross your legs at your ankles. You can rest your head on your calves. Fold your hands together at your bottom. Try to keep your feet behind your neck. Relax. Stay in this pose as long as you can without straining any part of your body. Now unfold your legs from your head, and lie flat on your back with your arms by your sides.

"This is a very relaxing pose."

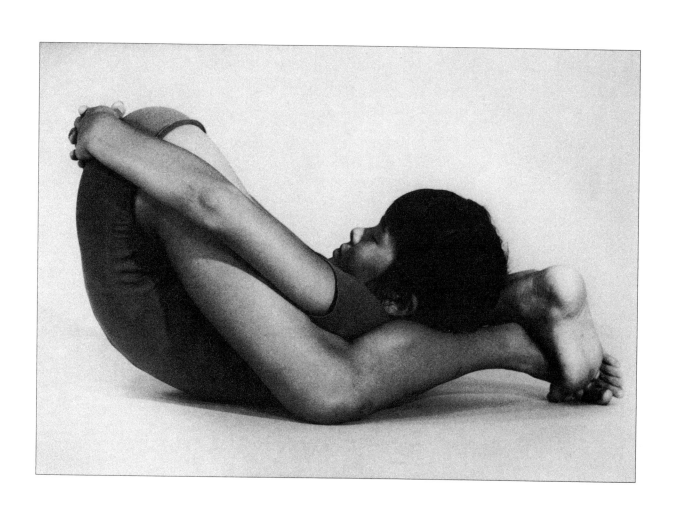

YOGA NIDRASANA - YOGIC SLEEP POSE _____ *85*

Section IV

MEDITATIVE POSES

MEDITATIVE POSES

When trying to meditate, you should sit very still with the spine straight and your eyes closed. You can pick one of these poses and practice sitting still in it a little longer every day.

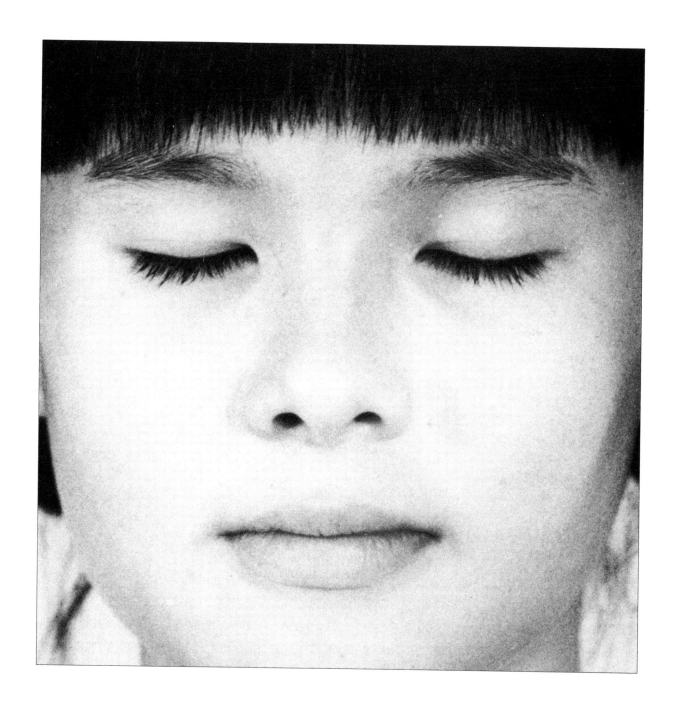

PADMASANA - LOTUS POSE

Please sit up with legs straight out in front of you. Put your right foot on your left thigh so that the top of your right foot rests on top of your left thigh and the sole is turned up. Now put your left foot on your right thigh with the sole up. Your right leg should be under your left leg. Pull your back up straight, and fold your hands on your lap, or put your hands on your knees. Have your head upright and centered. Close your eyes.

If you cannot do the full Lotus Pose, you can try Half-Lotus with one leg up on top of the other thigh and the other foot tucked under, or you can sit in a comfortable cross-legged position.

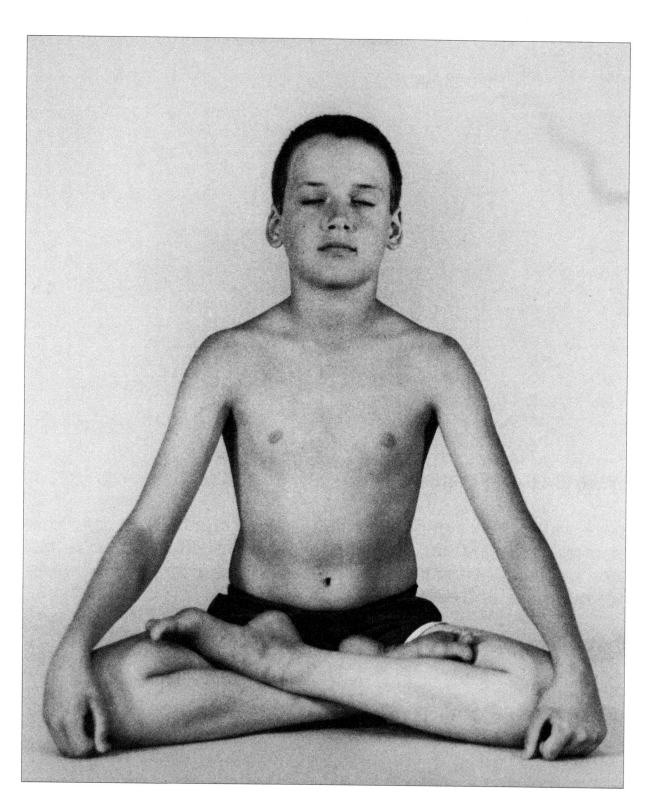

PADMASANA - LOTUS POSE _____ *91*

VAJRASANA - PELVIC POSE

Kneel on the floor, keeping the knees close together. Do not sit directly on heels. Instead, sit on the inner sides of your feet. Have the toes together and the heels apart. Then put the palms of your hands on your knees, and relax...

This pose is great for your digestion and for meditation.

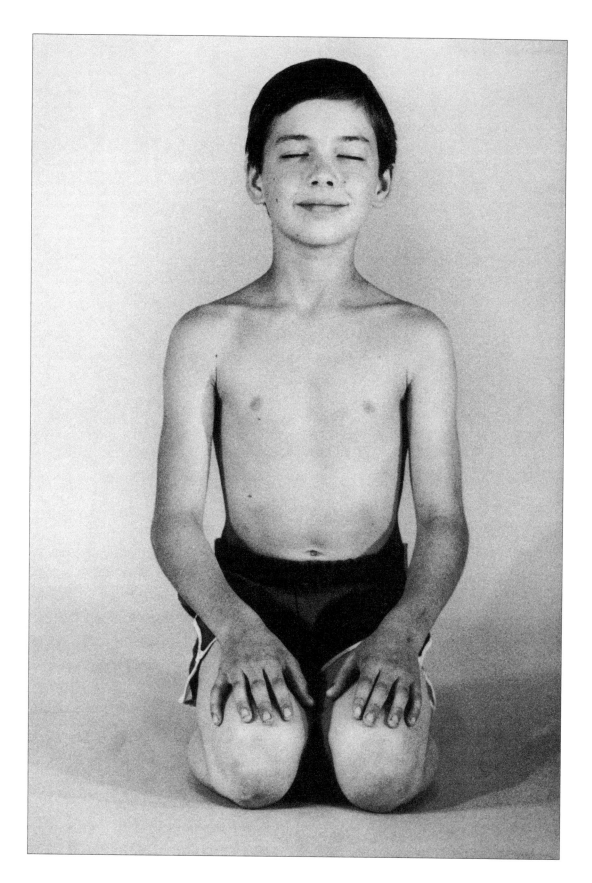

VAJRASANA - PELVIC POSE _____ 93

VEERASANA - HEROIC POSE

Sit on the floor, and fold back the left leg so that the foot is next to the right thigh. Now bend your right leg over your left leg. The knees should be on top of each other. Keep your heels touching your thighs. Make sure your back is straight. Clasp your hands together between your knees. Stay in this pose however long you would like to.

This pose stretches your legs and makes you feel good!

VEERASANA - HEROIC POSE _____ 95

SRI SWAMI SATCHIDANANDA

Sri Swami Satchidananda is one of the most respected spiritual teachers and Yoga masters in the world. A leader in the interfaith movement, he exemplified the precepts and the goal of Integral Yoga. His approach to teaching Yoga was direct, practical, and simple. His delightful sense of humor reminds us that the purpose of spiritual life is joy.

Sri Swamiji is the founder/spiritual head of Integral Yoga International and Satchidananda Ashram-Yogaville in Virginia. He is also the inspiration, designer and guiding light of the Light Of Truth Universal Shrine.

In 1978 Sri Swami Satchidananda founded the Yogaville Vidyalayam (Temple of Learning) or Integral Yoga School, which is located at Satchidananda Ashram-Yogaville, Virginia. He also founded Satchidananda Jothi Niketan (SJN), a residential school in South India in 1997. These schools educate children in the principles of Integral Yoga, such as truth, non-violence, spirit of dedication, and universal brotherhood, as well as academic skills.

For more information about Yogaville Vidyalayam, please contact Satchidananda Ashram-Yogaville, Buckingham,Virginia 23921and Satchidananda Jothi Niketan, Kallar Post, Mettupalayam, Coimbatore District 641305, India.